Bible Study in Duet

BOOKS BY CHARLIE AND MARTHA SHEDD

To help you manage your life . . .

The Fat is in Your Head
Time for All Things: Ten Affirmations for Christian Use of Time
Devotions for Dieters

For young people . . .

The Stork is Dead
You Are Somebody Special (edited by Charlie Shedd)
How to Know If You're Really in Love

On marriage . . .

Letters to Karen: On Keeping Love in Marriage
Letters to Philip: On How to Treat a Woman
Talk to Me
The Best Dad is a Good Lover
Celebration in the Bedroom (coauthored with Martha Shedd)
How to Stay in Love (coauthored with Martha Shedd)
Bible Study in Duet
Prayer in Duet

For parents and grandparents . . .

You Can Be a Great Parent
Smart Dads I Know
A Dad is for Spending Time With
Grandparents: Then God Created Grandparents
    and it Was Very Good
Grandparents' Family Book
Tell Me a Story: Stories for Grandchildren and
    The Art of Telling Them

Ideas for churches . . .

The Exciting Church: Where People Really Pray
The Exciting Church: Where They Give Their Money Away
The Exciting Church: Where They Really Use the Bible
The Pastoral Ministry of Church Officers
How to Develop a Tithing Church
How to Develop a Praying Church

Cassette Resource Kits . . .

Fun Family Forum
Straight Talk on Love, Sex, and Marriage
Good Times With the Bible

Bible Study
in Duet

Charlie and Martha Shedd

PYRANEE
BOOKS

Zondervan Publishing House
Grand Rapids, Michigan

BIBLE STUDY IN DUET
Copyright © 1984 by The Zondervan Corporation
Grand Rapids, Michigan

Pyranee Books are published by Zondervan
Publishing House, 1415 Lake Drive, S.E.,
Grand Rapids, Michigan 49506

Library of Congress Cataloging in Publication Data
Shedd, Charlie W.
    Bible Study in Duet.

    1. Marriage—Religious aspects—Christianity. 2. Bible—Study. I. Shedd,
Martha. II. Title.
BV835.S47   1984   248.4   84-20911
ISBN 0-310-42380-5

Edited by Anne Severance

Printed in the United States of America

84 85 86 87 88 89 / 10 9 8 7 6 5 4 3 2 1

Contents

Foreword

Bible Study in Duet is Charlie and Martha Shedd at their best. They attack two central problems of married life—communication with each another and communication with God. What is the point of establishing channels of communication between husband and wife if there is no life-enriching message to fill the channel?

This book contains no fancy dreamed-up theory of how to read and understand the Scriptures. Rather, it offers a practical, down-to-earth approach that ordinary people can use to mine the r.ches of biblical treasures and at the same time avoid the vicious cycles of conversational selfishness.

Do not think, however, that this method requires exhaustive concordances, multivolume commentaries, and erudite textbooks on biblical interpretation. It only requires a person to honestly mark the margins of the biblical texts with three different symbols: a candle ("A great idea"), a question mark ("What does it mean?"), and an arrow ("It hits me, so I better take it seriously"). Then once a week, or even more often, a husband and wife set aside time (1) to share the insights they have marked with candles, (2) to note the passages with question marks and decide how to find answers, and (3) to confide in each other the issues signaled by arrows and to help each other discover solutions. Now anyone can do that, if, as Charlie and Martha point out, a person is willing to talk and to listen.

Bible Study in Duet is not a scheme for foul-ball interpretations based on individualistic biases. Honesty about the question marks will inevitably lead readers so seek for reliable answers in various resource books: commentaries, Bible dictionaries, and Bible encyclopedias. Furthermore, as one continues to study the Scriptures in this realistic and sensible way, there is a self-correcting process that guides one out of stagnant lagoons of muddied thinking and into the central stream of biblical understanding.

Anyone who has had the privilege of knowing Charlie and Martha and of sitting under their ministry, as Althea and I have, will immediately recognize the refreshing insightfulness of their approach to biblical truths. When Charlie preaches, the Bible comes to life. One senses that the Scriptures have been listened to, talked about, shared, and lived.

Charlie and Martha have two great gifts: helping people become true families of God and making the Scriptures speak with authority and appeal. In *Bible Study in Duet* they have richly combined these two God-given talents.

Dr. Eugene A. Nida

Former Executive Secretary for Translations for the United Bible Societies of the World

Consultant for Translations for the American Bible Society

Acknowledgments

The authors and publisher are grateful to the following publishers for use of copyrighted materials.

AMPLIFIED, taken from *The Amplified New Testament.* Copyright © 1954, 1958 by the Lockman Foundation. Used by Permission.

GNB, taken from the *Good News Bible, The Bible in Today's English Version.* Old Testament: Copyright © American Bible Society 1976; New Testament: Copyright © American Bible Society 1966, 1971, 1976. Used by permission.

KJV, taken from the King James Version of the Bible.

LAMSA, taken from George M. Lamsa, *The Gospels from Aramaic,* Holman. Copyright 1933.

LB, taken from *The Living Bible.* Copyright © Tyndale House Publishers, Wheaton, Illinois, 1971. Used by permission.

NASB, taken from the *New American Standard Bible.* Copyright © The Lockman Foundation, 1960, 1962, 1963, 1968, 1971, 1972, 1973, 1975, 1977. Used by permission.

NEB, taken from *The New English Bible.* Copyright © The Delegates of the Oxford University Press and the Syndics of the Cambridge University Press, 1961, 1970. Reprinted by permission.

NIV, taken from the *Holy Bible, New International Version.* Copyright © 1978, New York Bible Society. Used by permission of Zondervan Bible Publishers.

PHILLIPS, reprinted with permission of Macmillan Publishing Co., Inc., from J.B. Phillips: *The New Testament in*

Chapter I

The Dream

Part I

Happy is the couple whom the Lord instructs.

Psalm 94:12

*Happy is
the couple whom
the Lord instructs.*

How close are we now to our original dream of the perfect marriage?

Good question any time for any couple. But for the Christian husband and wife there is an even more important question:

How close are we to the dream our Lord dreamed when He brought us together?

Would He rate us higher today than one year ago? Five years past? Twenty?

Is there any way to be sure our marriage is growing in its divine potential? Are there certain secrets to a no-fail union?

We think the answer is yes, and one of these certain secrets for us has been "Bible Study in Duet."

So this is our claim, our promise, the exciting news from forty years' experience—

Any couple who will commit themselves

together for a life-long sharing of

God's Word will be brought to exciting

new discoveries in their love

plus exciting new discoveries with the Lord.

How could this happen? The answer is that Bible Study in Duet brings with it two basics of marriage at its best. And the first of these is

TALK, TALK, TALK

What are the three most important words in any marriage?

"I love you"?

"You are beautiful"?

"Please forgive me"?

15

All ultra important. But our nomination for the three most important words in any marriage:

TALK, TALK, TALK

Why? Because without talk, talk, talk, "I love you" will not come through. Neither will "You are beautiful" nor "Please forgive me" nor any other of the basics.

From both sides we hear these noncommunication complaints, "My husband won't talk." . . . "You've heard of the sphinx? Well, I married it." . . . "There he sits! The great stone face." . . . "If all the silent husbands of the world were laid end to end, it would be a good thing."

In workshops, personal consultation, letters, phone calls, casual conversation, same sad lament from lonely wives. Less often, but still too often, same low moan from a puzzled husband.

Ask the average engaged couple, "What do you like best about your relationship?" Almost always, high on the list of answers is some song of praise to their communication. "We can talk about anything" . . . "No hiding places" . . . "I can tell him everything I'm thinking" . . . "Super sharing."

So what happens to these open roads?

To be sure, some of the answers are psychological. But for us, and for most couples we know, there is another plain vanilla reason.

Time for talk gets away from us. Almost before we know it our priorities are rearranged. Secondaries take first place and we find we're becoming strangers.

• • •

Here then is another all-important question for every one of us:

*Happy is
the couple whom
the Lord instructs.*

*In our marriage how much time do we spend talking together
about the deeper things?*

How many minutes per week do we share what we *feel?*
How many hours do we spend discussing the goings on
inside?

If that is too sensitive for starters, ask it another way: How
many minutes in-depth communication (per week) do we
estimate for the average couple?

We've asked this question of husbands and wives by the
thousand:

> Eliminating budget, children, neighbors, relatives,
> weather, happenings, events, things you see on televi-
> sion, what you read in the newspaper—all these aside—
> how much time per week do you spend communicating
> in depth?

The answer: *Six minutes!*

There are ten-thousand-eighty minutes in seven days, and
the average couple is reporting six minutes on feelings.

An Eastern university conducted a professional survey on
this same theme. They asked one thousand couples: "How
much time do you spend each week in 'serious discussion'?
And you define the word *serious.*"

Their finding? Amazing coincidence—six minutes.

A statistical accident, chance happening, quirk of the
figures? Or could it be that no matter who is doing the
testing, no matter who is being tested, this is a fact . . .

In too many marriages

bridges have broken down,

the expression of real feelings,

sharing of all things serious

has been crowded out.

. . .

LISTEN, LISTEN, LISTEN

Those who have ears to hear
*Let them hear.**

. . .

Blessed is the marriage where both husband and wife

are learning the art of

TALK, TALK, TALK.

Blessed, too, are they who train themselves to

LISTEN, LISTEN, LISTEN.

. . .

In personal Bible study we adhere to the principle of
"escalating attention."†

Principle: Any statement of our Lord which appears twice,
we will read twice and ponder twice.

Three times? Triple attention.

Does He say it four times? Quadruple.

But some statements of Jesus are repeated again and
again. What do we do with these? These we inscribe on our
minds until they become a natural part of our thinking.

---

*Matthew 11:15, Matthew 13:9, Matthew 13:43, Mark 4:9, Mark 4:23, Mark
7:16, Luke 8:8, Luke 14:35

†Editor's note: For those interested in the origin of word combinations, the
principle of "escalating attention" is a term developed by the Shedds for their own
Bible study in duet. In workshops and in their writing, Charlie and Martha often
advise, "Your Bible study together will have more meaning and be more fun if you
develop your own vocabulary."

*Happy is
the couple whom
the Lord instructs.*

Wise, then, the couple who will consider eight times the words: "Those who have ears to hear, let them hear."

Modern translations open up new vistas:

The man who has ears to hear should use them!
Matthew 13:9 (PHILLIPS).

Be listening.
Matthew 13:43 (AMPLIFIED)

Let him who has ears, listen.
Mark 4:9 (WILLIAMS)

Take note of what you hear.
Mark 4:23 (NEB)

Be careful how you listen.
Mark 4:23 (PHILLIPS)

Give your minds to what you hear.
Mark 4:23 (RIEU)

Be sure you really listen.
Mark 4:23 (C & M)

Is there any Christian who would disagree with this statement: Jesus was the number-one communicator of all time?

There may be others who would argue that claim, but not the believer. Nearly two thousand years after His life on earth, He is still communicating. Still speaking. Still listening.

Why would the Great Communicator eight times emphasize and reemphasize the importance of listening?

One sure answer is that most of us too often have our focus wrong. In too much of our conversation, we operate on this delusion: Our thoughts are more important than the thoughts of others. Our words have the better sound. Our feelings matter more than their feelings. Our ideas take precedence over theirs.

Not so. Always, without exception, one hundred percent of the time, no variance—to other people, what *they* think *is* number one to them.

How can we reverse this human predicament? How can we break the cycle of conversational selfishness? Our answer: Bible study in duet.

As we share the Scripture, we learn to talk, talk, talk.

Through this talk, talk, talk, we sense an amazing fact. "My mate is honestly interested in what I think, how I feel, what I say. The Spirit of the Lord has touched our marriage with Divine concern."

But that is only half the miracle. Through Bible study in duet, His Spirit is reshaping *our attitudes.* More and more *we* really *do* care with His kind of caring. It actually *does* matter to us what our loved one thinks, feels, says. So because it matters, we listen. We hear what we have not heard before. We even hear what the older translations call "groanings of the spirit." Later scholars labeled these "mysteries," "whispers," "deeps of the spirit."

Does anyone know all the vocabulary of the Spirit? Of course not. But we know this. . . .

• • •

The more we are faithful to our Bible study in duet,

    That much more the Spirit comes to reshape

      our attitudes;

    He frees us to talk, talk, talk;

    He breaks up our selfishness

*Happy is
the couple whom
the Lord instructs.*

that we might truly listen, listen, listen.

Then He provides another all-important ingredient for maximum marriage.

"GRACE"

If I should show you who I am, and you don't like it, what have I left? Nothing. There I am, all the weaknesses, the strange, and the evil in me, all exposed!

Is there any couple anywhere, any husband, any wife who hasn't felt touches of this?

So here we are with another reason couples do not talk and listen—*fear!*

What is the answer? The answer is that beautiful biblical word *grace.*

Grace is theologically defined as, "The free, unmerited love and favor of God." Which being interpreted in everyday vernacular means, "God loves us not because we deserve it; not because we've earned it; He loves us because we're His!"

All-important questions for any marriage:

What is the grace quotient in our love?

Do you understand that I accept you as you are right now? Faults and peculiars and funnies and odds, show me all you want to show me. Tell me all you want to tell me. Whatever you've done, whatever you dream, past, present, future, facts and fantasies, you can count on my love.

This is grace, and only grace leads us to feel, "Surely the Lord is in this place. This is none other than the house of God and this is the gate of heaven."

Chapter II

The Christian's Base for No-Fail Marriage

*Happy is
the couple whom
the Lord instructs.*

No-fail marriage!

Sounds good, doesn't it? Good ring to the words. Good solid feel. But is there really any base for making marriage no-fail?

Our answer?

A clear-sounding "Yes"

—the Bible!

When we married forty-five years ago, we were already well acquainted with the Bible. We had heard it read in church, in Sunday school, even at family devotions. It had also been a part of our wedding—a beautiful white Bible.

So we had determined the Word of God would have a prominent place in our home. And it did. Every day we saw it on our nightstand. No way we could miss it there. We couldn't miss the other copy either—the one on our coffee table.

Yes sir! Yes ma'am! Ours would be a Bible-based home. . . .

There is an interesting story of a very old church in Mexico. Every Sunday as the people entered, they bowed to a crevice in the wall. There, beside the outside door, they nodded to the hole, and many of them crossed themselves.

Why? That was exactly what some reporter asked one day at a funeral. Curious, he began to inquire of the worshipers, "Why do you bow to this hole in the wall?" Nobody knew the original reason. But almost everyone said, "We bow because our fathers and mothers bowed, and crossed themselves. Our grandparents did. Everyone *always* bows."

More curious than ever, the reporter went back to his office and began an extensive research. Finally, in an old, old picture from the newspaper morgue, he found the answer.

There in that faded picture, beside the door, a crucifix was clearly visible! Since those days the old church had undergone complete refurbishing, and in the process of remodeling, the workmen had apparently plastered over the crucifix. Yet still today the people bowed, and some of them still crossed themselves—the reason long since lost.

So Martha and Charlie nodded to their Bibles. We nodded to the one on our nightstand and the one on our coffee table. Not quite so often we nodded to others on our shelves. And that's the way it was around our house for much too long.

Most of us believe our God is a personal God, and that is one terrific assurance. The Creator of our universe did not go away and leave us. After the days of His creation, He stayed around. For what? One reason: He stayed to congratulate Himself and see that it was good.

That's what we're told before chapter 1 of His Book is done. But as we read on, we discover another reason:

God stayed with us because He loves us.

Then as our New Testament begins, we see Him coming to share Himself, giving Himself completely for us . . . birth, crucifixion, resurrection, that we might know His living presence personally and in our relationships.

Amazing truth—

The same God who sets out His stars each night

He who says to the sun each morning,

"Rise, shine,"

This very same God is a personal God

He wants to be our God

And if we give Him a chance,

*Happy is
the couple whom
the Lord instructs.*

He will speak to us

He will meld us

He will bless us

He will make our marriage what it should be.

We have heard it said that year five is the bad year for marriages. Others point to seven or eleven. For us, every one of those first years had too many negatives. Sometimes they came with shouting and crying and loud banging. Sometimes they came unannounced on padded feet. And these for us were the real uglies, because they also left on padded feet. But in their going, always they seemed to leave behind more uglies—hurt and a sense of rejection—anger and slow burning—feelings unexpressed.

When we first began to sense that our love was heading for trouble, we made a decision. Since we weren't doing well by ourselves, we would ask the Lord for His help. And where better to get His help than directly from His Word?

So we made a commitment. Every day we would read the Bible together. We would agree on a book and then we would take turns reading one chapter to each other . . . every day.

How did that go? It didn't. How could that possibly go? One of us is up at the crack of dawn, sometimes earlier. The other barely believes in God before 8:30 in the morning and two cups of coffee.

Then, too, there were days we didn't see each other until the evening hours. So we would do our reading at bedtime? Great way to get ready for sleep. Fill the mind with good things. But if the mind is weary, the body tired, concentration level zero, commitment level also zero, what then? "What then" was a total collapse of one more good intention.

What can we do when our good intentions collapse?

We can quit. Give it up as a great idea which never got off the ground. Or if we're still believers, we can back up and come at it again. So once more we committed ourselves to daily Bible reading. But this time we altered our approach.

Because we were not synchronized in those early morning hours, we would have our quiet times at different hours. And we still do.

Every day for forty years, we've read our Bibles and had our quiet times . . . each at our own time.

Every week for two thousand-eighty weeks, we've come together (at least once) for sharing.* "What did the Lord say this week to you, to me, for us together?"

Chapter 3 describes the system we developed to make our Bible study in duet a major focus in our marriage.

---

*Every day? No exceptions? Of course, there have been exceptions, but very few. *Every* week? Very, very few exceptions. Almost zero. And the reason? The more we are faithful to Bible study in duet, the better our marriage goes. But that's only reason one. Reason two: the more we are faithful to Bible study in duet, the better *everything* goes.

Chapter III

Candles,
Arrows,
Question Marks

*Happy is
the couple whom
the Lord instructs.*

"Isn't it sacrilegious to mark in a Bible?" Surprising how many times we are asked this question. For us the answer is a resounding "No!"

The Charlie-Martha Bible study method is based on three specific marks:

CANDLES

ARROWS

QUESTION MARKS

Each morning as we read our Bibles individually, we underline and mark.

When we come to an entirely new thought, new insight, new light, we underline and put a candle in the margin—a candle for new light.

When we read something we don't understand, have doubts about, something we can't believe, we underline and place a question mark in the margin.

Then there are the places that convict us. These make us realize we are not what we should be. Here we underline and use an arrow in the margin. (We do not place arrows for each other. We allow each the dignity of discovering his/her own sins.)

CANDLE New light
        Fresh thought
           Something we've never see before
             Exciting!

QUESTION MARK
        I do not understand
        Vague
           Whatever could the meaning be?

ARROW This convicts me
        Points to a flaw

There is a weakness in me here
I am a sinner

Then once each week, sometimes more often, we sit together and share our marks. Straight out of God's Word comes the impetus for talk, talk, talk.

Where do we begin?

If one of us has a mark at the first verse in Chapter 1, we begin there. A candle? "This is a new thought to me. What do you think?"

Perhaps it's Chapter 5 before we come to a mark. Or there may be four marks in Chapter 3.

At the same verse one of us may have a question mark; the other, a candle. Here we help each other.

If we both have a question mark, we go to our commentaries. What does the commentary say? Biblical scholars give us more inspiration for talk, talk, talk. Yet this we learned early in our pilgrimage: What the Lord says to us is more important than what He says to the scholars.

That being true, we discuss our questions for our own conclusions before we go to the wise men.

Candles for enlightenment

Question marks for further study

Arrows for self-analysis.

Anyone who needs a psychiatrist should find a psychiatrist. But those of us who are wrestling only with oddities or neurotic trends, may require nothing more than the help of a friend. For us, Bible study in duet provides that caring friendship. In the interchange of arrows, we share our quirks and foibles. With the tender touches of love and with God's help, we unbraid some tangled skeins. We help each other and He helps us to a new peace.

*Happy is
the couple whom
the Lord instructs.*

If communication

    (real depth communication)

        is the key to marriage at its best

           AND

If it is true that God

    instructs and guides

        out of His book

then this has to be one no-fail

method for no-fail marriage.

           • • •

Why? Because by this system two great things are happening—

We are sharing* our discoveries with each other

    and with the Lord.

But this is only half the miracle.

    He is sharing Himself with us.

Now to some specific candles, arrows, question marks, with a thought-starter for each.

CANDLES FOR NEW LIGHT

*In the year that King Uzziah died,
I saw the Lord . . . high and lifted
up—Isaiah 6:1 (RSV).*

> Sometimes when things are hardest, we *do* see the Lord. What negative experience in our lives has brought certain positives?

---

*Sharing is the key word. Our dictionaries define *sharing* as: "Giving and taking" . . . "enjoying together" . . . "exchange of ideas" . . . "developing with another" . . . "accepting" . . . "sharing the good and the bad."

To see your face is, for me, like seeing the face of God—Genesis 33:10 (C & M).

What a goal! Are we reflecting the Lord for each other?

Avoid stupid arguments—Titus 3:9 (C & M).

Flash! Some things are not worth even the slightest fuss. Are we reserving our energies for the important differences?

We must not be proud or irritate one another—Galatians 5:26 (C & M).

Let us now have an honest sharing time on: "The thing you do that irritates me most."

Elkanah {her husband} answered {Hannah}, "All right, do whatever you think best"—1 Samuel 1:23 (GNB).

As far back as the Old Testament a fine part of a fine marriage has been the granting of individual freedom.

Where do we tend to box each other in?

Where would the ring of some liberty bell sound a plus in our love?

Would we have more genuine togetherness if we allowed each other more freedom at certain points?

ARROWS FOR CONVICTION

In quietness and confidence is your strength—Isaiah 30:15 (LB).

In times of rush, rush, rush, are we learning to listen for the still small voice?

Happy is
the couple whom
the Lord instructs.

Do the noises of this world steal too much of our sharing time?

I will help you to speak, and I will
tell you what to say—Exodus 4:12
(GNB).

What a promise—a promise for every public contact, and a promise for our sharing with each other. Are we letting the Lord bring us to a fuller sharing?

That's enough! Don't mention this
again!—Deuteronomy 3:26 (GNB).

Should we write this verse on our minds for touchy subjects, embarrassing moments, delicate matters, certain historical boo-boos?

And I sat among them, overwhelmed,
for seven days—Ezekiel 3:15 (LB).

Always, getting behind the scenes in other lives prepares the way for more understanding, more love. Do we honestly try for the other person's view?

Don't hide your light. Let it shine
for all—Matthew 5:16 (LB).

Do we tend to let our light shine for people outside the home and fail to turn it on for each other?

Men, you should have listened to
me—Acts 27:21 (LB).

If ever a verse applied to us, this is it.

"I told you so" . . . "Didn't I warn you?" . . . "Why didn't you pay attention?" . . . Shouldn't these lines be on our "never-say" list?

QUESTION MARKS

The Lord called me before my birth.
From within the womb he called me
by my name—Isaiah 49:1 (LB).

What do these words mean to us: "Sacredness of life
. . . "the rights of the unborn"?

With all the talk about abortion these days, do we
have a solid theological position here?

For the eyes of the Lord search back
and forth across the whole earth—
2 Chronicles 16:9 (LB).

Is this an awesome warning or a beautiful promise?

As a couple, are we doing anything we'd rather the
Lord did not see?

For it is written, "As I live," says
the Lord, "every knee shall bow to me
and every tongue confess to God."—
Isaiah 45:23 (C & M).

Can this be true?

When . . . ?

The Bible has it all. Every subject we need to discuss,
every problem we need to face, every place we need to
grow—it's in The Book. That being true, every couple who
will commit themselves to Bible study in duet is sure to
grow, to be taught, to be entertained. And one certain
reason is that God speaks to us out of His Word as He
speaks nowhere else.

All this is why we call the Bible—solid base for no-fail
marriage.

Chapter IV

Meditations

*Happy is
the couple whom
the Lord instructs.*

When we have discussed our candles . . .

When we have faced up to our arrows . . .

When we have worked through our question marks . . .
we find it especially helpful to listen quietly together for a
time. When we do this prayerfully, we can almost hear the
Lord saying, "Now that you have had your discussion, here
are some questions straight from Me!"

We share now some more of the Lord's questions to us.

Each of the following meditations came together like this:
One of us marked the verse with which the meditation
begins. Following our discussion we quieted ourselves and
listened. Then came more talk, more ideas, more surfacing
of selves, more questions. As noted, somehow for us these
questions that seem to come from the Lord have about them
an awesome holiness. "Holy" in the sense of "whole";
"wholeness" . . . "constituting an undivided unit" . . . "sound
and healthy" . . . "complete" . . . "total."

Our hope is that, by introducing you to our methods, you
will work out your own methods. But by whatever method
you develop, we know you will find this true—

> If you will include some listening time together at the
> passage, some waiting together,
>
> you *will* hear Him!

Then when you follow even the smallest light He gives
you, He will lead you to more light.

A word fitly spoken is like apples of gold in a setting of silver—Proverbs 25:11 (RSV).

HOW GOOD ARE WE AT SAYING "THANKS"?*

We will think now of our marriage as an old-fashioned scale—on the left, negatives; positives on the right.

Most of the time our scale tips   right ☐
                                       left ☐

We will set aside time for thanksgiving now. We'll make a list of things (about each other) for which we are grateful:

_____

_____

_____

Thoughts on gratitude from a California husband:

I am writing you because this is Thanksgiving month, and I want to tell you what happened to my wife and me last year about this time. Up until that time our marriage was only average, and some of the time below average.

For the first year or two we had a good thing, but then it began going downhill. The reason was that we had fallen into the habit of putting each other down.

This year when school was out for the holiday, we sent the children to visit my wife's parents. Then later she and I drove to their home for Thanksgiving dinner and to bring the children back.

I don't know who thought of it, but on that drive one of us suggested we start telling the things we were grateful for, the good things that had come our way during the past year.

---

*Illustrations for this section have been selected from two sources: (a) the letters we receive; (b) input from our Fun in Marriage Workshops.

Happy is
the couple whom
the Lord instructs.

Then my wife began to tell me some things about me she was thankful for. Wow! This was something new. So I told her some, and it had been a long time since we had exchanged compliments. We could hardly believe this was happening.

Well, the whole thing was absolutely great. In fact, it was so great we decided that from then on we would do it more often—like every week.

Since then, we've hardly missed a week, and we both agree this past year is the best year we've ever had.

We thought maybe there might be some other couples who would like to hear what happened to us. Like I said, just telling each other what we are thankful for does make a difference, and especially it does if we keep it up.

Assignment: This week we will go to the commentary and count how often the words *thanksgiving* and *gratitude* are mentioned in the Bible. Then we will select seven of these verses and discuss one every day for seven days.

Sensible people will see trouble coming, and avoid it, but an unthinking person will walk right into it and regret it later—Proverbs 27:12 (GNB).

DO WE OVER-RESPOND TO EACH OTHER'S MOODS?

Subjects and happenings which tend to depress the mood in our marriage are: (Check one or more.)

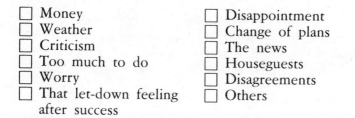

☐ Money
☐ Weather
☐ Criticism
☐ Too much to do
☐ Worry
☐ That let-down feeling after success

☐ Disappointment
☐ Change of plans
☐ The news
☐ Houseguests
☐ Disagreements
☐ Others

Who sets the mood around here? Do I "go down" when my mate is down?

Comes now an interesting letter from Iowa. Joe is a high school teacher. His wife is an accountant, and from Joe's report, they must have an unusual relationship.

Thelma is a beautiful person, but she's one of those moody people—up one day and down the next. This hasn't always been easy, but lately I decided to do something about it.

I used to get up in the morning waiting to see how Thelma felt, and then I felt like she felt. If I sensed she was feeling good, I'd feel good. If she was out of sorts, I'd be out of sorts, too.

But not anymore. I came to the conclusion that this was ridiculous. Why should I let her determine how I was going to feel? So now I ask myself, "Who sets the mood around here?" Then I decide how *I* feel.

*Happy is
the couple whom
the Lord instructs.*

Almost immediately I began to see some changes, because Thelma started reacting to my feelings. She noticed it right away, too, and even thanked me. It is almost as if she needed direction and was waiting all this time for me to take a position so she could follow.

Anyway I can tell you since I decided to take the lead, things have been a lot better for both of us.

Then there is one thing more. I also began to notice a difference in my classroom. It was as if my opening tone not only affected my whole day, but the students' as well.

What couple couldn't profit from a discussion of Joe's question: "Who sets the mood around here?"

But now I tell you: anyone who looks at a woman and wants to possess her is guilty of committing adultery with her in his heart—Matthew 5:28 (GNB).

CAN WE HONESTLY DISCUSS OUR TEMPTATIONS?

For us, this beautiful line from Longfellow is another goal in our love:

> Straight between them ran the pathway,
>
> Never grew the grass upon it
>
> Singing birds, that utter falsehood
>
> Story tellers, mischief-makers,
>
> Found no eager ear to listen,
>
> Could not breed ill-will between them,
>
> For they kept each other's counsel,
>
> Spake with naked hearts together.*

Check one:

In our marriage are we hiding more and more from each other? Yes _____ No _____

Are we moving toward more thorough surfacing of all our feelings, including the ultra-sensitive? Yes _____ No _____

From a tempted husband:

Do you know anyone who ever cheated on his wife without getting caught? I have heard of men who say they did, but it

---

*The Song of Hiawatha, sc. VI, ll. 8–15.

*Happy is
the couple whom
the Lord instructs.*

seems that everyone of my friends who tried wound up in a
peck of trouble, and I don't want that.

Most of the time my wife and I have a pretty fair thing
going. But that doesn't mean you never think of anyone else,
does it? Right now someone is throwing it at me, and to be
one hundred percent honest, I'm thinking it over.

What I really wish is that I could talk to my wife, but we've
never been that open. So that's what I'm asking, "Does
anyone ever get by? No problems?"

A most unusual letter, and he must be a most unusual
person to be so honest. But that unusual honesty is the very
reason he wouldn't be getting by even if he had that one
hundred percent clandestine affair.

In the long run people as honest as he is will respect
themselves more if they are honest all the way.

The honesty questions come often. "Should we always tell
all?" "When?" "How?"

Caring mates learn the art of timing. Some days it takes all
the strength we have just to go on breathing. To unload at
low energy levels might be devastating.

We're also wise to ask this caring question: "Would it hurt
my mate more right now to hear it all than it would hurt me
to carry it by myself for a time?" In most marriages the
Golden Rule of Jesus is without equal.

But the fact still stands: Total honesty is a goal toward
which we must keep our love moving. Any husband and wife
studying the Bible in duet will hear it over and over:
personal honesty, honesty with each other, honesty before
God is the ultimate.

I tell you, whenever you did this for one of the least important of these brothers of mine, you did it for me!—Matthew 25:40 (GNB).

ARE WE DOING ENOUGH FOR OTHER PEOPLE?

Would we love each other more if we took more time to love other people?

1. In our marriage are we really "other-oriented?"
   Yes _____ No _____

2. How much thought, time, effort, money do we give to the needs of people outside our home?

   _____

   _____

3. What could we be doing in our neighborhood, community, state, the whole world to make things better for somebody who needs what we could give?

   _____

   _____

Thoughtful story from a lady in New Hampshire:

Most of us have been residents here a long time, and I suppose like they say about New Englanders, we are a bit standoffish at first.

A year ago this fall, a new couple moved in across the street from us. Of course, I took the usual plate of cookies over and found out a few things about them. They came from South Carolina. I didn't ask why they moved here, but I had my own thoughts.

Happy is
the couple whom
the Lord instructs.

Our winters are sometimes severe, and this winter was no exception. Anyhow, we all noticed a peculiar thing. The wife did their snow-shoveling, carried the wood for their fireplace, and ran most of their errands. I guess we wondered about that, because her husband was a big, strong, healthy-looking man.

Now I almost hate to tell you. In February, the husband died, and naturally we all went to visit the widow. Then we learned the full story. He'd had a serious heart attack and doctors agreed his condition was inoperable. This made it necessary for him to take early retirement. Since the house belonged to an old aunt, they could live here rent-free.

Why am I writing you? Maybe this is my way of going to confession. All that time, we were doing nothing, and we are ashamed of what we didn't do. We're even ashamed of each other. My husband and I agree we would be feeling better now if one of us had said, "Come on, let's extend ourselves a little."

Fine words for improving relationships at home and other places: "Come on, let's extend ourselves a little."

*But seek ye first the kingdom of
God and his righteousness; and all
these things shall be added unto
you—Matthew 6:33 (KJV).**

*Do not give what is holy to dogs
... Do not throw your pearls in
front of pigs—Matthew 7:6 (GNB).*

ARE WE SPENDING TOO MUCH TIME WITH TV?

"Where are we spending too much first-class time on second-class items?" In our workshops, this two-letter answer comes through like a flashing red light:

TV

What difference does it make how many hours we spend watching TV?

Here is a letter which says it well:

We have a question for you. It is a question we ask ourselves regularly and we pass it along. There might be other couples who need to ask: Are we falling into the trap of believing that, because there is a lot of talk going on at our house, we are really communicating?

This is our story:

We have been married three years and, at first, things were good. Then lately we realized something was wrong. It seemed somehow we were losing touch. No, it wasn't that we were angry, or afraid to talk, or not spending time with each other. It was rather that we just were not getting things said.

Well, we sat down to analyze and we found the trouble all right. The trouble was our TV. At breakfast, it was our

---

*As we go through the Bible together, one verse brings to mind another. We have learned to be particularly attentive when this happens. For us double direction may be doubly effective, as in the verses above.

Happy is
the couple whom
the Lord instructs.

favorite newscast; in the evening when we got home from work, the news again. After dinner, it was back to the tube for our regular programs. Weekends, too, a lot of TV— games, golf, even church services.

You can see there was plenty of talk, but it wasn't talk *between us.* In one of your books you wrote that we need to check whether we are communicating, not only with our heads, but with our souls, too. Well our problem was all eyes, and too little soul as in "Too much television!"

When we located the trouble, we determined to make some changes in our lifestyle. We decided to set aside time for talking about important things and for getting our feelings across to each other. I guess you would say we made the decision that there is nothing on television as important as what goes on between us.

Always this is super loving: Face facts, analyze what's wrong, and then do something to make things right again.

In any way does this story apply to us?

Love is not ill-mannered—1 Corinthians 13:5 (GNB).

Love is never rude—1 Corinthians 13:5 (LB)

WHAT IS OUR COURTESY QUOTIENT?

Essay on "What Makes Marriage Great" (by small girl):

> I think to make marriage great you have to treat each other like company a lot of the time and be polite and stuff like that.

• • •

How much difference would it make in our marriage if we gave more thought to treating each other like company and "stuff like that"?

For "please" . . . "thank you" . . . "excuse me" . . . and other phrases of common courtesy, we grade each other (zero to 100) _____.

Do we sometimes treat other people better than we treat each other? Yes _____ No _____

Words of a young wife:

> I am slowly losing respect for my husband. Why? He's becoming so careless about his personal habits. Sometimes I think he is almost vulgar. I've talked to him about this and told him he's turning me off, but I don't think he hears me. Is there anything I can do?

Words of a young husband:

> I'm getting worried about my wife and what she is becoming. I don't like to say it, but sometimes she's downright crude. Never a "please" or a "thank you" anymore. I know things are different today from the day I grew up, but shouldn't manners be "in" for every generation?

Happy is
the couple whom
the Lord instructs.

There's one sad truth in life I've found

    While journeying east to west,

The only folks we really wound

    Are those we love the best.

We flatter those we scarcely know,

    We please the fleeting guest.

And deal full many a thoughtless blow

    To those we love the best.

(Author unknown)

• • •

From Genesis to Revelation the Bible bears down hard on this fact: Real religion is tested by our treatment of others. Shouldn't this especially include those at our own address? For further development of the theme, see chapter 5, page 67.

I confess my sins, I am sorry for what I have done—Psalm 38:18 (LB).

I'M SORRY

1. The last time one of us apologized was

---

2. Have we discussed thoroughly why it may be hard to apologize? Yes _____ No _____

3. When one of us apologizes, the other accepts that apology graciously. Yes _____ No _____

4. Does either of us tend to be a bit pious? Yes _____ No _____

According to our mail, resistance to apology is a common problem.

This letter comes from Illinois, but what the lady says might have application anywhere.

My husband has a very hard time admitting he is wrong. All the men in his family are like that. So it meant something special to me when you wrote in *Letters to Karen* that it doesn't matter who starts the fuss. What matters is that someone will start the apologies.

It was almost uncanny that I read those words at a time when we were into a big one. He wouldn't give in, and I wouldn't. So I asked myself, "How do we get out of this?"

Then I got an idea. I wrote him a note and, before he left for work, I slipped it in his pocket where I knew he would find it. Now, you should understand, I still felt he was more wrong than I was. He even admitted that later, but what I said in the note was:

I am honestly sorry we aren't getting along.

*Happy is
the couple whom
the Lord instructs.*

Please, can't we be friends again?

That's all I said, and would you believe when he found my note, he called me to tell me he wanted to be friends again, too. He said he was as sick and tired of the fuss as I was. Then he even said he was sorry—two or three times! That might not sound like much to you, but if you knew him, you'd know it was a miracle.

I thought maybe you'd like to know about this. I really think it's true that the most important thing is not who is to blame, but who will start somewhere trying to make things right again.

A nagging wife is like water going drip-drip-drip on a rainy day— Proverbs 27:15 *(GNB).*

DOES ANYONE AROUND HERE NAG TOO MUCH?

In our marriage workshops one theme sure to raise its ugly head is "nagging." We find it wise on occasion to do some personal research on frequently asked questions from other marriages.

Is there a specific point in our relationship where we should quit nagging? Yes _____ No _____

One of us? Yes _____ No _____

Both? Yes _____ No _____

Who's most prone to nag?

This little verse for wives (Proverbs 27:15) certainly must include the badgering husband, too.

Psychologists tell us almost all nagging comes from background factors. The mind experts also say many of the problems in any relationship started long before that relationship began. If they are right, then knowing the ancient origin of any problem will have a positive effect on any marriage.

Assignment: Individually and together we will consider places where we tend to nag. Then we will try to track these to their origin and discuss our findings.

Letter from an appreciative wife:

I thought you might be interested in something which happened with us. For several years I've been twenty pounds overweight. Sometimes thirty. Wally's reaction was to nag, and the more he nagged, the more I ate. Well, three months ago on my birthday, he wrote me a nice note in which he told me he was giving me an unusual gift. His gift was *that he would never say another word about my weight.*

Now that was really something for Wally. In fact, it was sensational coming from him, because, as long as I can remember, he's been on my case. So now he said he was through, and I can still hardly believe it. Sure, he slips sometimes, but when that happens, all I have to do is look at him a certain way, and he tells me he's sorry.

Can you guess what happened?

When I saw he really meant it, something changed in my attitude. I decided I would try my best to make him the gift of a wife like the one he married. No, it hasn't been easy, but I'm determined, and I've lost fifteen pounds. I still have several more pounds to go, only now I feel confident that I'm on the right road. Some day I'll get it off. There is simply no way I can tell you what this has meant to both of us.

Three more words to go along with *talk, talk, talk, and listen, listen, listen —*

hush, hush, hush.

I will drive them out little by little by little—Exodus 23:30 (GNB).

ARE WE EXPECTING TOO MUCH TOO SOON?

The children of Israel were sometimes impatient. Their leaders were forever calling them to understand that the Promised Land could not be reached in one giant step. "Little by little"—these three words can become a motto for our relationship. In serious Bible study we hear this note again and again.

Examination for patience factor:

1. Do we push too hard sometimes for changes and corrections? Yes _____ No _____

2. In order to better both myself and our relationship, I am willing to change, but in these areas I feel you pressure me too much:

_____

_____

_____

3. Can we agree on one place (or several) where we should begin easing off?

_____

Jerry and Sue had come for counseling. The very fact that they were having trouble surprised them. Theirs had been an ideal courtship. Everyone said they made a perfect couple. But now, only a few months down the road, things weren't going well.

In all the flow of their talk, Jerry kept returning to this one-liner, "I guess we expected too much too soon."

*Happy is
the couple whom
the Lord instructs.*

Many of us make that mistake. We assume that, by the mere act of mounting those chancel steps, we are climbing heaven's stairs.

Yet those of us who have been married a long time know it isn't that way. The heavenly marriage is more like a kit to be put together slowly, carefully. Sanding, fitting, gluing, hammering, varnishing, waxing, polishing. "I do" does not mean "we did it."

One of our friends is a hobby craftsman. He carves mottoes with his router and he makes interesting plaques of his favorite sayings. Most of his mottoes are done on polished board, pine, mahogany, walnut, oak, maple. But one he inscribes on tough-looking boards from the beach or from an old barn. And that motto is:

Radishes mature in a few weeks.

Oaks take years to grow.

Chapter V

Talk-Starters On Some Major Problems

*Happy is
the couple whom
the Lord instructs.*

"Where do we start?"

"Will you give us some suggestions for launching talk, talk, talk?"

These, and many other questions, come to us through the mail, in workshops, from dialogue of every kind.

In Chapter 5 we shared certain verses with their expanded meditations.

Following now are what we call "talk-starters."

These, too, come from our own private collection of helpful texts. Each began with one of our candles, arrows, question marks. Each has contributed to our love.

ANGER

Let all bitterness, and wrath, and anger, and clamour, and evil speaking, be put away from you
—Ephesians 4:31 (KJV).

There will be flashes of anger in even the best relationships. Do we need to develop a more effective way to handle hostility when it surfaces? How can we "put away" these things of Ephesians 4:31?

Additional verses for meditation:

Proverbs 15:1   Matthew 12:25

Romans 12:19   James 1:19–20

Our own thoughts on these verses:

_____

_____

_____

_____

_____

_____

_____

_____

_____

*Happy is
the couple whom
the Lord instructs.*

FAITHFULNESS

> *Be thou faithful unto death, and I
> will give thee a crown of life—Rev-
> elation 2:10 (KJV).*

Some scholars say God is promising a crown to those who
will be forever loyal. But isn't our loyalty to each other a part
of our loyalty to Him?

Are we absolutely loyal to each other? Verbally?

Are we thoroughly committed to physical fidelity?

Additional verses for meditation:

Genesis 2:23 (Matthew 19:5)

Ephesians 4:29

Our own thoughts on these verses:

_____

_____

_____

_____

_____

_____

_____

_____

_____

FORGIVENESS

> *Therefore as God's people consecrated, and dear to Him ... be merciful ... just as the Lord has freely forgiven you, so must you do also—Colossians 3:12–13 (phrases from* TWENTIETH CENTURY, KJV, *and* WILLIAMS*).*

Does either of us tend to carry a grudge?

Or do we both harbor hurts too long?

What can we do to live more like genuine

Christians at this point?

Additional verses for meditation:

Matthew 5:7

Matthew 6:14

Matthew 10:21-22

Our own thoughts on these verses:

_____

_____

_____

_____

_____

_____

_____

_____

*Happy is
the couple whom
the Lord instructs.*

JEALOUSY

> *Wherever you find jealousy and rivalry, you also find disharmony and all other kinds of evil—James 3:16 (PHILLIPS).*

In any way are we in competition of a negative nature? Are we mature enough to face these problems, discuss them, and then surrender them to the Lord?

Do we know where our jealousies originate?

Other verses for meditation:

Galatians 5:26

1 Corinthians 13:4

Our own thoughts on these verses:

_____

_____

_____

_____

_____

_____

_____

_____

_____

MONEY

> *Be not highminded, nor trust in uncertain riches, but in the living God, who giveth us richly all things to enjoy*—1 *Timothy 6:17 (KJV).*

Are we too much concerned with money?

Does it dominate us?

Would we do better with a better philosophy of spending, saving, giving?

Additional verses for meditation:

Ecclesiastes 5:10	Luke 6:38
Malachi 3:10	2 Corinthians 9:7

Our own thoughts on these verses:

_____

_____

_____

_____

_____

_____

_____

_____

_____

*Happy is
the couple whom
the Lord instructs.*

PRAISE

> *A word at the right time is like
> apples of gold in a network of sil-
> ver*—Proverbs 25:11 (C & M).

For compliments, praise, and verbal affection, our rating
is:

Superior _____

Average _____

Low _____

Zero _____

Are we satisfied with things as they are?

What could we do to improve?

For meditation together:

Song of Solomon

**Our own thoughts on praise to our lover from this
beautiful psalm:**

_____

_____

_____

_____

_____

_____

_____

SELFISHNESS

> *Love does not insist on its own*
> *way—1 Corinthians 13:4–5 (RSV).*

Would ours be a better marriage if we disciplined ourselves to think *first* of our mate?

Are we growing in the unselfish love described throughout all of 1 Corinthians 13?

How can we become more Christlike in our concern for each other?

Other verses for meditation:

Matthew 7:12 and Luke 6:31

Romans 12:10

Galatians 5:13

Our own thoughts on these verses:

_____

_____

_____

_____

_____

_____

_____

_____

Happy is
the couple whom
the Lord instructs.

TROUBLE

> *The Lord is good, a strong hold in*
> *the day of trouble; and he knoweth*
> *them that trust in him—Nahum*
> *1:7 (KJV).*

Anyone can smile when success is certain and the sky is blue! But what will we do when the shadows come?

Will the troubles we face drive us apart or draw us together?

Additional verses for meditation:

Psalm 30:5	Psalm 138:7
Psalm 46:1	Romans 8:28

Our own thoughts on these verses:

_____

_____

_____

_____

_____

_____

_____

_____

TRUTH

> *You desire honesty from the heart
> ... sincerity ... truthfulness—*
> Psalm 51:6 *(LB).*

On a scale of zero to one hundred, our grade for absolute honesty with each other is _____

Since the Lord desires honesty from the heart, are we growing in that direction?

Additional verses for meditation:

John 8:32

Philippians 4:8

Our own thoughts on these verses:

_____

_____

_____

_____

_____

_____

_____

_____

_____

_____

_____

Chapter VI

Texts For
Minor Matters

*Happy is
the couple whom
the Lord instructs.*

In the previous chapter we dealt with certain majors which seem to surface in almost every marriage.

Here we present themes, Scriptures, questions heard less often. Yet are they really minor?

Word from ancient sage:

There is no such thing as a minor problem

   if it's a problem.

IN-LAWS   GENESIS 27:46 (GNB).

In-law conflicts are as old as the Old Testament.

> *Rebecca said to Isaac, "I am sick and tired of Esau's foreign wives" (see also Genesis 26:34).*

Questions:

If our in-law relationships are on the plus side, do we praise the Lord enough for this good gift?

If negative, have we really talked it through, listened it through to a workable philosophy?

Lord, thank you for our in-laws!

Lord, help us understand and appreciate the larger family!

Happy is
the couple whom
the Lord instructs.

RETIREMENT   NUMBERS 8:25

Compulsory retirement laws are no new thing.

In great detail, the Book of Numbers, chapter eight, sets forth laws for the temple and temple workers. Verse twenty-five says of the Levites:

> *At age fifty, they must retire from their regular service and work no longer—Numbers 8:25 (NIV).*

In one of our trips through the Old Testament, both of us marked a candle at Numbers 8:25. In so many trips, we had completely overlooked this verse on previous readings.

New light! Plus all-important questions:

What can we do to help others ready themselves

for retirement?

Thank God for new work laws more equitable

to older citizens. Can we add our voices for

even more sensible rulings?

What about our own attitudes toward retirement? Are we looking ahead wisely, planning ahead wisely, saving wisely?

Lord, help us with the far look!

COMMITMENT   **1 KINGS 3:3**

Half-hearted religion is no new thing.

Arrows at 1 Kings 3:3 point to this ever-so-human
tendency—we follow the Lord, but only part way.

Surrender, yes! But limited surrender. This verse says it
clearly—

> *Solomon loved the Lord, but he burned incense to other gods*
> *(C & M).*

Interesting study—check how many times this verse, and
others like it, appear in the annals of Old Testament kings.

But who are we to point the finger?

Lord, help us to

continually examine

our own commitment!

*Happy is
the couple whom
the Lord instructs.*

NATURE   JOB, CHAPTERS 38–41

*What holds up the pillars that support the earth? ...
Who closed the gates to hold back the sea? ... Who makes
the hills and valleys stand out like the folds of a garment?
... Do you know how clouds float in the sky? ... How
the sky is swept clean by the wind? ... Who waters the
dry and thirsty land, so that grass springs up? ... Who
is it that feeds the ravens? ... Who made the horses so
strong, and gave them their flowing manes? ... A golden
glow is seen in the north and the glory of God fills us with
awe—excerpts from Job chapters 38–41 (adapted from
Good News Bible).*

On every trip through our Bibles, these chapters of Job ask
their questions again to our blessing. They fill us with
wonder. They tune us to the world around us. They cause us
to exclaim with the psalmist, "O Lord, our Lord, how
excellent is thy name in all the earth."

The CANDLES of Job point to fresh insights.

ARROWS point our negligence.

QUESTION MARKS ask us again:

Are we responsive enough, grateful enough for the
lavish love of God manifest in nature?

SLEEP   PSALM 127:2

He giveth his beloved sleep (KJV).

Interesting how often we hear the "sleep" complaints—

Seems as if we simply cannot get our inner tuning synchronized. One of us is early to bed, early to rise. The other is late
to bed, late to get up. You think it's funny! Well, we did too
at first, but year after drifting year, it's one more way we're
drifting apart.

Would you believe! Every night right after dinner he
turns on the TV, sits in his big chair, goes sound asleep.
Whenever does a woman communicate with a sleepy-
head like that?

She says she needs eight hours sleep, or ten, and no way can
she hold her job without it. I tell her she could train herself
to get by with less if she'd only give it a try. I work too, you
know, and I only need six hours; sometimes five does me.
You can't believe how we fuss over sleep.

and on and on and on. . . .

Would some serious meditation on Psalm 127:2 be a help
to us?

Does God give to all alike?

How long has it been since we both had a physical
checkup?

If we trained ourselves to some quickie naps, would that
be an aid to our blending?

If we shared more of the home responsibilities, would this
alleviate that tired feeling?

What kind of "rest" compromises can we work out and
work in?

What, other than sleep, do we do for relaxation? What
could we do?

*Happy is
the couple whom
the Lord instructs.*

And for some entirely new terrain on the sleep themes, maybe we should discuss these added words from another translator:

"He giveth *to* his beloved *in* sleep!"

CHEERFULNESS   PROVERBS 17:22

> *Being cheerful keeps you healthy. It is slow death to be gloomy all the time.* (GNB)

True for individuals.

True for two together.

Would our marriage be a healthier marriage if we concentrated on being cheerful?

Are we facing the things which make for gloom in our relationship?

Do we take time to laugh at life and enjoy each other?

Additional verses for our meditation:

Psalm 134:34

Ecclesiastes 3:13

John 15:11

*Happy is
the couple whom
the Lord instructs.*

SILENCE

MATTHEW 27:12, 14
MARK 14:61; 15:5
LUKE 23:9

Sometimes silence is golden. Sometimes silence is plain yellow. Everyone knows that to keep still when we should speak up can be damaging to a relationship. Yet shouldn't we also know that sometimes (temporarily maybe, permanently maybe) no answer is the right answer.

Here, in several references from the trial of Jesus, the message comes through loud and clear, "When there is nothing to say, say nothing!"

Do we need to discuss how and when we could be more Christlike in our tense moments?

For additional study:

How many times does the Bible give us this three-word admonition:

"Hold your peace!"

FRIENDSHIP

JOHN 15:14
EPHESIANS 5:3–7
1 JOHN 3 AND 4

Arrows—arrows—arrows, with some pointed questions on friendship:

> *Proverbs 18:24*
>
> *Would we have more friends if we were more friendly?*
>
> *Ephesians 5:3–7*
>
> *Are we running with the wrong crowd, drifting into negative relationships?*

For some serious talk, talk, talk between us:

How do we take our stand without being pompous?

Are we mature enough Christians to reject

the wrong but love the wrongdoer?

Are we getting out of our church the full

potential of friendship in the family of God?

> *(1 John 3 and 4)*

Important questions needing important answers.

Perhaps we should read all of these references

again . . . and again . . .

Now above all—

How are we doing with the Friend of friends?

> *Ye are my friends, if ye do whatsoever I command you—*
> *John 15:14 (KJV).*

*Happy is
the couple whom
the Lord instructs.*

JUDGMENT   PSALM 141:3 (KJV)

We know one husband and wife who, together, are forever putting others down. No one escapes their censorship. Everyone says they are a bore, and they bore us too. Yet welcome to the club, Charlie and Martha. Right here, aren't we judging "the judgers"?

Judgment is like that—it breeds more judgment—it's sinister—we do it without knowing we're doing it—it's also habit-forming.

Shouldn't we as a couple run frequent checks on the negative things we say about others?

Like a constant metronome the Bible sounds this note:

Matthew 7:1–5	Romans 2:1
John 7:24 and 51	Titus 3:2
John 8:7	James 3

Set a watch, O Lord, before my mouth,

Keep the door of my lips.

Chapter VII

A Few Old Friends

Happy is
the couple whom
the Lord instructs.

There are those who enjoy looking up Bible verses for their own special needs and inspiration. For these, we include now a section based on some of our favorites. Each reference here has made significant contribution to our own growth in communication.

One of the exciting things about God's Word is its ability never to give up. A particular verse may convict us on our first trip. Next time, it turns on a bright light. Trip three raises questions. Reading four may give us the feeling that a neon light is flashing many signals.

We have included here spaces for personal thoughts and new ideas. Often, in the columns of our Bibles, we write a few words describing current reactions and add the date. At the next reading these words may serve as a window to something we'd missed before.

The following examples were selected at random.

After thirty trips through the Old and New Testament, a wonderful thing happens. Almost every page and each chapter is like an old friend.

Meet now a few of our old friends.

NEHEMIAH

Those who make a serious thing of Bible study in duet will create their own favorites from The Book. One such for us is Nehemiah. Candles, arrows, question marks *beaucoup.* Every page replete with marks. From our own study we have selected here one verse from each of the thirteen chapters of Nehemiah. (Lines are for personal thoughts and comments in duet.)

1:4 _____

_____

2:2 _____

_____

3:5 _____

_____

4:9 _____

_____

5:19 _____

_____

6:2 _____

_____

7:2 _____

_____

8:10 _____

_____

9:21 _____

*Happy is
the couple whom
the Lord instructs.*

10:36 _____

11:2 _____

12:42 _____

13:14, 22, 31 _____

PSALM 90–97

Some weeks our dialogue covers several chapters. This section of the Psalms, like many passages, has much material for discussion. So much new light, so many arrows and question marks, so loaded with thoughts for sharing.

90:14 Arrow _____

_____

_____

91 Star (See chapter 8, page 99) _____

_____

_____

92:1–2 Candle _____

_____

_____

92:11 Arrow _____

_____

_____

94:12 Candle and Question Mark _____

_____

_____

96:13 Question Mark _____

_____

_____

*Happy is
the couple whom
the Lord instructs.*

MATTHEW 6:25–34

On some occasions our weekly session may never get beyond one small section of a single chapter.

Verse 25: Arrow, candle, question mark*

_____

_____

Verse 27: Question mark

_____

_____

Verse 28: Candle

_____

_____

Verse 31: Question mark, arrow*

_____

_____

Verse 34: Question mark, two arrows*

_____

_____

---

*Sometimes from a single verse we do get new light, conviction, and a question or two, plus arrows.

JOHN 21

Another chapter with many marks for our discussion is John 21.

Verse 6: Question mark

_____

_____

Verse 10: Arrow

_____

_____

Verse 25: Candle

_____

_____

Verses 15–19: Candle, arrow, question mark

_____

_____

Chapter VIII

Questions and Answers

Happy is
the couple whom
the Lord instructs.

Our Fun in Marriage Workshops are divided into
three sections. One of these is Soul Communication
where we deal at length with Bible study in duet. In
this chapter we deal with the questions most frequently asked following the Soul Communication
session:

1. *Where is a good place to begin Bible study in duet?*

We do not think it's wise to start with Genesis and work
straight through the Bible. In some marriages one is more
biblically advanced than the other. But starting with Genesis, even the most experienced could become discouraged.
All those lineages, the fighting, the cruelty, the hate passages
might be a bit much. For us a good launching pad in the Old
Testament has been the Psalms, or Proverbs. The Gospels
make a good starting place in the New Testament. And who
could go wrong beginning with 1 Corinthians 13?

2. *Do you recommend that we both use the same translation?*

Some of our most productive times have come from using
different translations. Right now one of us is reading the
Bible in Basic English which limits itself to 850 words. The
other is reading Lamsa's Translation based on the Syriac
rendering of the Greek original. The variance here is
fascinating—the simplest—the most erudite. For us, it's like
looking through a wide lens telescope.

We think one of the best modern translations is *Good
News for Modern Man*. Both scholarly and simple, this is the
work of the American Bible Society. Since the American
Bible Society is part of the United Bible Societies of the
World, scholars are brought in from everywhere. The clever
little drawings scattered throughout the text help us "see"
meanings.

We try to keep up on all the new translations and
incorporate these in our study. Particularly with our question mark verses, we find it helpful if we refer to the newer

translations. Comparing this fresh insight with older versions invariably opens up new thought.

One of the newest versions we're using for supplemental insight right now is our own publisher's *The Holy Bible: New International Version*. Compiled by more than one hundred scholars, no serious student of Scripture could fail to be stimulated to think new thoughts.

3. *Is there a difference between a version and a translation?*

No, there is no basic difference between a version and a translation. The word *translation* is the more modern usage, while *version* is the more traditional term. However, today they mean the same thing.

4. *Is it true that the King James version is nearer to the original than any other? I was brought up in a Sunday school where there was something special about it. What do you think?*

No question—it *is* special. For beautiful phraseology the King James simply cannot be duplicated. However, after using many versions and translations, we have concluded that some of these newer versions are closer to the original. Makes sense, doesn't it? In every field experts are continually coming closer to the truth.

Our catechism tells us the Bible was written by "good men taught of the Holy Spirit." Christians believe that the Holy Spirit is every bit as active today as yesterday. Contemporary scholars can be and are channels of His ever-growing truth.

5. *Should we skip some passages?*

Yes, at first. Later on you may prefer to read from cover to cover. As we study for help with problems and moods, we soon learn what passages lift and bless. When we ask for His guidance, the Lord will lead us to verses, chapters, whole sections which meet our special needs for special times.

6. *In using your system, what if one gets too far ahead of the other?*

*Happy is
the couple whom
the Lord instructs.*

There is a built-in safeguard in our approach. When either of us has finished a book, we wait for the other to complete it. In our case one of us is a naturally fast reader; the other, slow, making flexibility important. It is never our intent to proceed together, chapter by chapter. On any given day one of us may read only a few verses. The next day we may take two chapters, or five. Our weekly sessions keep us somewhere in the same general range.

7. *Do you think it's important to read books about the Bible before we begin with the Bible itself?*

No. We think it's important for serious students to read books about the Bible, but not before beginning the Bible itself. Books on "how the Bible came to be" can provide excellent background. Books on individual books of the Bible are also helpful. Since individuals have different needs and different couples have different needs, too, we recommend browsing through Christian bookstores. Most of these carry a line of materials on the Bible. The term we use for this general reading and study is "our helicopter ride over biblical terrain." In no way, however, is the helicopter ride a must before getting directly into God's Word.

8. *Will you give us some thoughts on commentaries and other helps?*

For those who wish to go deeper, individual commentaries are available on each book of the Bible. Or if you prefer the simple approach, there are some excellent one-volume commentaries covering the entire Bible. There are many Bible dictionaries which will make good additions to any library. Advice from your pastor or browsing again in your bookstore may be helpful in the selection of commentaries and other aids.

9. *How long will it take us to go through the Bible together?*

There are 1,189 chapters in the Bible. Beginning with Genesis and reading through Revelation will take a little over three years reading at the rate of one chapter per day.

We don't set that kind of pace. Our speed has varied from reading through the Bible in two years to much longer.

Because we are all so different, there is no definite answer to the "how long" questions. Yet since there is no prize for speed, hurrying is not imperative. What is imperative is that we stay with our reading faithfully and take plenty of time to talk, talk, talk and listen, listen, listen.

10. *What if we make a mistake in interpreting Scripture? Couldn't this be dangerous?*

We don't think so.

If we are into ongoing Bible study, God has a way of correcting our errors. He leads us from the byways back to the main road. We can count on the biblical promise, "If it is of God, He will bless us. If it isn't, He'll protect us."

11. *Do you ever use other marks in addition to the candle, question mark, and arrow?*

Yes, but the candle, question mark, and arrow are our special marks, our own original development by us for us. Yet, are they ours? Ecclesiastes 1:9 tells us, "There is nothing new under the sun" (RSV). That, statement, by our experience, is much more than the observation of an Old Testament cynic. Almost everything has its duplicate in some day long gone.

After we began our marking system, we discovered other similar systems, mostly historical. From monks and nuns in the middle ages we learned of their methods. From more current groups in other lands—Sweden, Italy—we read of their developments, their approaches also based on certain marks.

But yes, we have some subsidiary marks we use sometimes:

> *Thumbs down*—Negative. Isn't this the antithesis of a Christian attitude?

*Happy is
the couple whom
the Lord instructs.*

Exclamation point—startling . . . unusual!

Star—ultra-important . . . don't ever forget it . . . write it on the heart, the mind.

Plus mark—for some positive note we need right now.

Rippled lines at the side—read these sections to get the meat of the coconut.

How often do we use these subsidiary marks? Not often. If you were to look through the Bibles on our shelves, you would find thousands of candles, question marks and arrows, but only occasionally other marks.

12. *Two comments from our mail:*

Whenever we sit down to talk about the Bible, my husband has all the answers. He doesn't pay attention to what I think. Why? Because he thinks he's so brilliant. How long would you study the Bible with someone like this?

What if you're married to a woman who's a real know-it-all?

Very sad. Basic principle for Bible study in duet: We must respect each other's right to individual interpretation. We must encourage new ideas and fresh thought from our partner. Wonder of wonders, the more we allow for God-given individuality, the more we grow in God-given oneness.

And isn't this respect for individual insight right on target to this Scriptural claim—God hides some of His wisdom from the wise that He may give special insights to the simple?

Here are some questions for those who suffer with the heavy-hammer types:

Is there some psychological reason why my

mate must dominate?

And is there any way I can lead this "I-know-more-than-you" character into consultation either with me or with a professional?

13. *Do you keep a record of your discussions?*

Yes, some thoughts we file. But the most important record is right there in our Bibles. Every day, in our reading time, we write the date. This way the Bibles on our shelves, marked and dated, become a record of our spiritual pilgrimage.

14. *Do I understand correctly that your Bible sharing is a feature of your weekly dates? (See "Our Weekly Date" in chapter X.)*

No. Our weekly dates are times for soul blending on a different level, for romance, for fun, and for all sorts of interrelating not connected with study.

The sharing of our marks is most often done at home on our rocking loveseat. Occasionally this may be in the early morning; sometimes it's in the evening when our energy levels happen to be up. It might be on the weekend. Another interesting "when and where" for us is in the car. Almost all of us spend time together riding somewhere. What a way to go! The four-wheeled chapel!

15. *Wouldn't it be a good idea to include the whole family in Bible study?*

Yes, and those interested in further thoughts on family devotions will enjoy our book, *You Can Be A Great Parent.**

. . . One more time. For married love at its absolute best there is no substitute for Bible study in duet.

---

*You Can Be A Parent, Charlie and Martha Shedd [Word, Inc. 1970], pp. 74–77.

Part II

A word in
due season,
how good it is.

Proverbs 15:23 (C & M)

Chapter IX

On the Making of Time

*A word in
due season,
how good it is.*

"Whatever happened to our love? We used to be so close, so together. And now it's like the old song, 'Where Have All The Flowers Gone?' "

Straight from one of our marriage workshops comes this inner moan of a young husband. And when he had spent himself in sad soliloquy, he came at last to his summary phrase:

> *I think I know the answer. We're too busy, plain run over in the zip, zam, and zowie.*

Switch now to another classic. This from a lonely housewife:

Dear Dr. and Mrs. Shedd,

Jerry and I used to be such good friends. At least that's how I remember it, and he says he remembers it that way, too.

I do think that's how it was. Before we married, one of the great things we had going was the way we could discuss everything. I do mean everything, our hopes and our hurts, our love for each other, things we liked and didn't like, our guilt, everything.

So what happened? One thing that happened is three kids. Do you know what that means? What that means is time consumption, almost total time consumption. Car pooling, music lessons, bumps, bruises, fussing, fighting, little questions, little answers, big questions, big answers, and on and on forever.

But that's not all. There are neighbors to keep up with, friends to see, and oh yes, our jobs! I forgot to mention we both work. Jerry is sales manager for his company, real good at it, but he gets so tired. I'm a nurse, also real good at it, and I get tired, too.

So we come home, and wouldn't we like to sit down to talk, to hold hands, share, make love? But there is dinner to cook, dinner to eat, dinner dishes to do, meals to plan for

105

tomorrow, house to straighten, homework, phone calls, and have you ever counted all your evening interruptions?

So we fall in bed, Jerry and I. Fall? That's exactly the right word—fall, as in fall exhausted.

Then in the morning it's do it again. Breakfast, lunches to pack, schedules to check, dinner to plan, good-byes, "take care," "I love you," plus a million more last-minute "this's and that's."

So what's the matter with weekends? Please don't mention weekends. Last weekend, like so many other weekends, was total disaster. And that disaster, sorry to say, centered entirely in the church.

Yet we can't give up our church. That wouldn't be right for the children, plus we have so many friends in our church. Only sometimes I wonder, Does our church really know how harassed and hurried we are?

Anyway, I tell you true, sometimes I could just cry the way Jerry and I look at each other. It's almost as if some lonesome part of us was calling, "You seem like such a nice person over there. I wish I could know you. I mean I wish I could know you again."

I'm sure Jerry feels like I do, because we really do love each other; at least the last time we had a moment to discuss it, we loved each other. Yet sometimes I wonder—all this waving at each other, shouting across a chasm, how long can it go on? What if we're dangerously close to becoming strangers?

What if *we* are?

*A word in
due season,
how good it is.*

THE BIG DELUSION

Nomination for major mistake. Mental error number one.
Big delusion in most marriages:

> *Some day off in the future, darling, we will stumble onto
> big chunks of time. When we get caught up a little . . .
> when the car is paid for . . . when we work the mortgage
> down a bit . . . when we get another promotion, save more
> . . . when the kids are a little older . . . when the strain is
> off . . . then we can relax . . . then we will take it easy,
> travel, have fun, just be together.*

So what happens?

What happens is that we arrive at our fancied ease, and
where is the ease? These days are crowded, too. Crowded
with "muchness" and manyness," and where have all the
flowers gone? We have been chasing another chimera, living
by the big delusion.

Conclusion:

We never will *find* time!

Time for important things

Time for building friendship

Friendship with each other

Friendship with the Lord

This kind of time is never *found*

This kind of time is only *made!*

And among the greatest makers of time is Bible study in
duet.

Chapter X

So How Can We Make Time?

*A word in
due season,
how good it is.*

The word covenant is loaded with special meaning for all religious people. Dictionaries define *covenant:* "Agreement between two or more" . . . "a compact" . . . "contract" . . . "pledge taken together."

When we marry, we covenant to love, honor, cherish and provide for. Some of us even promise to obey, and all of us promise to be faithful.

Good promises, every one! But are they good enough?

No!

One graduate school professor, a real wag, would start us off on test day with, "Define the universe and give three examples." At which we would smile and then move to question two.

Some things are so all-encompassing we can only nod and say, "Yes. Of course. I agree." And for the two people we know best, the marriage covenant is very much like that. Too grandiose. Too massive. Too, too far removed from plain vanilla everyday concourse.

So whatever can we do?

One thing we can do is to live the major covenant of marriage by many little covenants.

OUR WEEKLY DATE

Early in our years together we took this pledge:

> *By whatever means required, we will not let our love be crowded out. Come success, come children, come urgent matters of every kind, nothing matters more than our togetherness. That being true, once each week (at least once) we will go from our home for an old-fashioned "date." A time of romancing. A time for fun. A time to dream, and a time to remember. But above all, this is our time for in-depth communication—sharing our love by talk, talk, talk. Sharing our love as we listen, listen, listen.*

Score on this commitment?

One hundred percent. Forty-five years times fifty-two weeks equals two-thousand-three-hundred and forty weekly "dates." Who wouldn't be best friends after investing that much time?

What if we had to miss one week? Then we made it up the next week, or the next. No excuses. None.

Usually we managed a dinner date. But some busy weeks when there simply were no evenings, we would book a lunch together. Some fine restaurant? Occasionally, but never in the early years. Then, and even now, it was and is more likely a favorite simple place. And in those years when the budget was super tight, we would sometimes make it a long walk; a drive, if we could afford the gas; maybe a picnic in the park.

(Interesting note: The more we grow in love, the simpler grow our tastes. Why? Isn't this because the real thing is not outward decoration? Wherever we're together, the decoration is exactly as it should be. And what we're sharing on our date is not first sustenance for the body, but food for the soul.)

*A word in
due season,
how good it is.*

Never did we count those times when we were entertaining or being entertained. Our dates were *our* time for talk, talk, talk. Our time to put our elbows on the window sill of heaven and gaze deep into each other's souls.

So this is another major answer to "How can we make time?" *The weekly date.*

Subquestion: What's the matter with regular sharing time at home?

Answer: Nothing. Great idea. But for us, too often across the years, this is one more great idea murdered by a gang of brutal facts. Facts like the telephone. Facts like the doorbell. Facts like children, large or small. Facts like a light bulb needing replacement, or the hot water heater going out, or "Will you help me with my schoolwork?"

Interruptions we have always with us. That being true, for us, week by week, year by year, there is only one answer. This is the regular observance of a regular special event for regular sharing of our love outside the home. No exceptions. No excuses. A sacred covenant for talk, talk, talk, listen, listen, listen.

OTHER LITTLE COVENANTS

HAPPIEST MOMENT

"What was your happiest moment today?"

If every day toward evening (dinner . . . after dinner . . . bedtime), you agreed to share your number-one recall of that day's good happenings, would that be a plus for you?

At one of our workshops a loquacious psychiatrist, when he heard about "happiest moment" made this statement:

> *Did you ever figure how much of your dinner talk, your after-dinner talk, and even bedtime talk focuses on the negative? I tell you what, for Ginnie and me this "happiest moment" thing has to be one super idea, one sure winner. And what a way to go to sleep!*

Was it something like this Paul meant when he wrote, *Love rejoices not at wrong, but rejoices in the right.—1 Corinthians 13:6 (RSV).*

What would it mean to our marriage if we were to really bring these words alive in our love?

Little covenant for major miracle:

What was your happiest moment today?

HOW OTHERS MAKE TIME

EARLY MORNING COFFEE KLATSCH

The Martins live in Virginia. They're a busy couple with three teenagers. He has a good job in the local garment factory. She works at the bank, and this is their story.

> We've been married twenty-one years and you know what they say? The bad times come in multiples of seven. We really don't believe that, because almost every year for us has had its bad times. Lots of good times too, fortunately. But isn't it sad the way those bad times tend to dominate?

A word in
due season,
how good it is.

Well, to be perfectly honest, this year we woke up to some
real slippage. I mean certain happenings we knew couldn't be
anything but bad unless we moved in on them right now.

To make a long story short, when we took an honest look,
we knew why these things were happening. The reason was a
breakdown in our communication. Why? I'll tell you why. It
was three teenagers—eighteen, fifteen, thirteen. Do you
know how many things three teenagers can be into? Football,
drama, clubs, friends, rock music, country music, band music,
chorus, church, dating, one broken arm, one broken heart,
grades good and bad, and believe me that's only for starters.

So, in all this chaos, how could the two of us ever find time
for being alone with each other?

Well, we found a way and we thought we should write and
tell you in case there are other couples with our problem, or
some other problem like it.

What we decided we would do is to set our alarm thirty
minutes early every morning. I mean every single morning
we wouldn't even leave the bedroom till we had spent one
solid half hour together just plain visiting, listening, sharing
our love. (I take the coffeepot to the bedroom at night, ready
to plug in). We started this three months ago, and there is
simply no way we could tell you what a difference it has
made. We both feel this is going to be our best year ever.

Repeat. Say it again. One more time.

Any way we do it

   Creating time for talk, talk, talk

      listen, listen, listen

   Starts us on the road to our best year ever.

MONDAY NIGHT FOOTBALL FORUM

Dear Dr. and Mrs. Shedd:

Last night after the children had gone to bed, my husband sat me down and told me about an unusual gift he was going to give me. He said this year he was going to give me the first half of every Monday night football game. Not just this week, but every week, he and I would just visit during the first half.

Now that might not sound like much to you, but you see he commutes, so he doesn't get home till 7:30, sometimes later. Every Monday night for years it's been the same routine. I would feed the children early. Then Bob and I would sit by the TV and have our dinner. At first he tried to explain football to me, but I never really could appreciate it, and I think the reason is I wanted to talk. I wanted to hear about his day, to tell him about mine, just plain visit.

Well, I wish you could have heard the speech he made when he told me what he was going to do. Believe me, it was one of the most beautiful things I ever heard. He told me he had been thinking about football and us, and he had decided two things. First, he said he decided it couldn't be good for the children being shoved aside while he watched football. But the best part was the next thing he said (and I know I will appreciate this forever), "In the second place, Lucy, after being with the kids all day, you must need some scintillating conversation, and you know how scintillating I can be." I guess you can see why I'm so thrilled and why I say I think I have the greatest husband ever!

Aside to the male gender:

Why do we think we have to do some big, big thing to make our love what it should be?

A trip to Hawaii, that mink stole, the new home. If only we could manage one of the biggies, then she would love me like crazy.

But would she?

116

A word in
due season,
how good it is.

Probably not.

The Book says,

Behold how great a matter

a little fire kindleth—James 3:5 (KJV).

HIGH-TECH TALK

Are you ready for this? The Johnsons do most of their talk, talk, talk by cassette recorder. Excerpt from his letter:

Right now we're going through a period when we're absolutely snowed, and I do mean snowed. I'm at the height of my career, and this is the year it's go-for-broke. But would you believe that is exactly how it is with her? She's one rung below the top of her ladder, too, this year. But we do love each other, and as you know, we both love the Lord.

So we took one look at this and decided there is no way we're going to lose touch with each other or with the Lord. Fortunately, we're crazy about our jobs, and even though it means go, go, go, traveling, long hours, we have actually communicated more this year than ever.

How? Are you ready for this? By cassettes. It's a great way to stay in touch, and here's how the idea started. One time when we were into one of our own discussions on what could happen if we weren't careful, we remembered one little item from one of your books.

It was about the couple who couldn't express themselves very well, so they talked by tape recorder. And that's exactly how we've done it. Every week we exchange cassettes. Never less than three cassettes. I mean three cassettes each. That's what we promised, and to date we haven't missed a single week.

In a lonely hotel room, in our car (we both commute), any open moment of the busy day we talk to each other, and I simply can't tell you what this has meant to us. It has freed us both to pour ourselves into our jobs without the customary guilt trip. And it's done a lot for those times when we are together, too.

Now I should tell you we both agreed this couldn't go on forever. But we also agreed we'd give it a try for one year and then we'd reevaluate.

Please do tell our story. Sure, it may sound weird, but we are praising the Lord for some unknown couple's brilliant idea.

Brilliant is the right word. Any time any couple can develop any method for talk, talk, talk, listen, listen, listen, there is only one word for this: *brilliant*.

EIGHT HUNDRED HOURS

If you and almost any other person had spent eight hundred hours visiting about everything, you'd be good friends, wouldn't you?

That's what my wife and I have done. We've spent eight hundred hours in what you call talk, talk, talk. Sounds impossible? It would be if you tried to do it all at once. But let me tell you how we did it.

Every Saturday morning for the seventeen years of our marriage, we've gone out to breakfast, just the two of us together. When the children were small, that Saturday morning baby-sitter money had top priority. Even when we had company for the weekend, we still did it.

Weren't there ever any emergencies and didn't we have to miss some Saturdays? Yes, but do you know what we did? We made it early Sunday morning before church. That's why I can say we have spent eight hundred hours visiting with each other. Actually, we could double that and not be far off, because many times our Saturday morning session goes on for at least two hours.

We teach the couples' class at our church and this is one thing we tell them. Don't give us any excuses for not taking

*A word in
due season,
how good it is.*

time to communicate. I'm a traveling man, gone five days a
week, and we do it. If you really want to, you can do it.

SANCTUARY ON THE CELLAR STEPS

Since all three of our children are junior high age, our house
is sort of like a zoo, if you know what I mean. Animals,
friends, telephone calls, and oh that loud music!

Arnie and I have always been good communicators, and we
thought you'd like to know one way we've kept it good. You
can see that with us it's not a matter of whether we're going to
talk, but where and when.

Some years ago when the house was total confusion and we
had a decision that had to be made, we went to the basement
steps. Well, from that day we've made it a practice to spend
some regular talk time there.

If anybody asks, How do you keep the kids from
interrupting? That's easier than you might imagine. We
simply told them this is our place, so unless it's an emergency,
you leave us alone. It's amazing how you can teach even a
small child to respect parents' privacy.

Anyway we call our cellar steps "our sanctuary," and that's
what it's been for us.

Chapter XI

Rewards of Bible Study in Duet

A word in
due season,
how good it is.

Talk, talk, talk. Say them again. Say them often. Say them loud and clear. These are the three most important words in any marriage.

Listen, listen, listen. Say these too again and again, clear and loud.

Talking together—listening together—this is the number-one plus for Bible study in duet.

But there are other blessings.

1. THE THRILL OF DISCOVERING TOGETHER

The zest and tang of fresh ideas, new thought, surprises. Since boredom is a serious threat to every marriage, Bible study in duet becomes a built-in guarantee against the "blahs." This is true, because the more we learn, the more we yearn to learn. New light on the Scripture, new light on ourselves, new light on our relationship—all these make for ongoing excitement individually and with each other.

2. SYMPATHETIC UNDERSTANDING

Inevitably, Bible study in duet leads to a clearer view of two interiors. Mate reactions which seemed peculiar now begin to make sense. Result? A growing sympathy. Compassion.

But that's not all. As we share the deep places, we discover similarities. See how many verses we marked with the same marks. Thank you, Lord, for sudden harmony sometimes, plus slow blending in Your Word.

3. RESPECT

Has our respect quotient eroded with the passing of time?

Bible study in duet provides a built-in safeguard against this sad demise. As we listen to our mate, we thank God. Such an incisive mind! See all these fine ideas, superior insights. Out of all the people in my world, see who I chose? Congratulations to me and how fortunate I am. Thank you, Lord!

4. WE BECOME MORE TEACHABLE

Why are some of the wisest folks we know among the humblest folks we know? One answer: The more we learn in any field, the more we realize how much there is to learn.

"He really knows his Bible." . . . "She is a fine Bible student." . . . How often we've heard these compliments.

*A word in
due season,
how good it is.*

Yet, if ever that kind of praise gets back to the one of whom it's said, he or she might comment: "What I know is nothing compared to what I know there is to know."

So this is another result of our study together, we become more teachable and how much nicer it is to live with someone teachable."

5. PHYSICAL HARMONY AT ITS MAXIMUM

So often in our workshops, in consultation, in letters, we hear the plaintive cry, "If only we had a better sex life, we'd have a better marriage." To which we reply: "You've missed the point. The point is that maximum blending of bodies requires maximum blending of minds and souls."

One more plus for Bible study in duet.

6. DELAYED BLESSING

Does the Lord have special angels whom He assigns to work in the unawareness?

You struggled with a problem. You prayed, and no answer came. The tension remained, conflict continued, there was no peace. Then one day without your knowing, you realized those clouds had cleared. It may have been weeks later, years later. Suddenly you felt an inner quiet. Somehow, below the surface, God had been sorting things out, putting them where they belonged, making them right.

It is our experience that the more we study together, the more His delayed blessings become reality. And can't we count on this same happening in the future?

The psalmist says, "My times are in thy hands." Won't that be true of tomorrow, too?

Blessed are they who have learned

that today's time,

times past,

times off there in the future

are His times too.

7. SURPRISE! WE ARE BETTER PEOPLE!

That is one great day when we can look in the mirror and say, "I really do like what I see." More than ever I can say again and mean it, "Congratulations to me!"

Yet isn't there one greater thrill? This is two of us saying together, "Ours is a better marriage than ever before. Spiritually we really are making progress. Congratulations again; this time to *us!*"

8. WRITING OUR OWN TRANSLATION

As we gain confidence in Bible study comes another exciting plus. The day arrives when we realize, "Here is a message straight from the Lord with our name on it." So this is the meaning of "C&M": To Charlie and Martha it comes through like this.

No serious students of Scripture will play loose with meaning or change texts to fit behavior. But this we can count on: If we commit ourselves to Bible study in duet, His message does come through with special meaning for us. No question. This is His personalized word for our duet.

9. INNOVATIVE TECHNIQUES

He brings from His treasure things
new and old—
Matthew 13:52 (c & m).

Innovative techniques

Fresh ideas

These, too, are rewards of Bible study in duet.

*A word in
due season,
how good it is.*

One such for us is what we call, "Release it! Let it go!"

Example—for some months there has been a disagreement between us. Small at first, we thought it might go away. Yet the hard fact is we're getting nowhere!

Give it to the Lord? Yes, but how?

Find a verse and let it go.

Process:

After having agreed we should table the matter, we find a verse which seems exactly right for this particular problem. Next, we write a brief description of the disagreement, perhaps in code. We date the note and place it at the chosen verse. Then we pray, "Lord, we're getting nowhere. We don't like it. We don't think you like it, either. We know you see problems of every kind. We know you see things about this problem we can't see. So here it is. We release it now to you. We leave it in your care. Thank you."

What do we do when we begin chewing on the problem again individually; chewing on it with each other? Back to the chosen verse we go and one more time we pray, "Lord, we really did mean to release it. So here it is again. Thank you for your patience with us."

Psychologists say we should never bury our disagreements. Too many times they push over old tombstones and shake their gory locks again. True. But for us, using the Bible to let our disagreements go temporarily can be a genuine healer.

Question: Do we ever sit together, open The Book once more and look at our problem together? Yes, when we both agree the time is right.

Amazing truth—sometimes when we go back for another look, this lovely fact comes clear. He has touched our problem with some warm memories. Or maybe He gives us some easy-to-understand directions, solutions we could never have seen or managed on our own.

All these "Release it! Let it go!" items are not in the conflict category. They may be burdens, worries, people problems, children problems, economic problems, job problems. These and many more of every trauma are for that all-inclusive invitation: "Cast thy burdens on the Lord."

Recently we had gone to our Bible shelf for reference in a particular translation. As we turned the pages, out dropped a slip of paper dated five years past. Because it was written in code, try as we might, neither of us could remember what this ancient problem was all about.

Review:

Find a verse; release it; let it go.

Step one: Write the problem.

Step two: Select an appropriate verse or passage.

Step three: Place the paper at that verse.

Step four: Pray a prayer of release.

Step five: Leave it with the Lord.

Step six: Review it again when we both agree.

Chapter XII

Witness from Bible Study Duos

A word in
due season,
how good it is.

In our workshops and correspondence, we frequently ask for reports from those couples who are studying the Bible in Duet. Here are some reports straight from where it's happening.

From California:

> Last August we made an in-depth study of the Book of Revelation together and in April we studied Paul's Letter to Galatians while on vacation. These moments of reading and studying the Scriptures together are the most precious moments of the day, and our love and devotion for one another grows deeper and richer as the years go by. Burdens are lifted, problems are solved, peace and serenity are experienced, and we feel God's Presence in these quiet times. We have read the Bible through together from Genesis to Revelation, using different translations, and find we must discipline ourselves to make and take time for study, for personal communication with God.—Ed and Fern

After a couples' workshop:

> Our marriage was in the process of strangulation from lack of communication, verbal affection and the glue that holds it all together—God. We'd gone from seminar to seminar, from counselor to counselor, and we seemed to be getting nowhere. Well, we thought, one place we haven't been is into the Bible together. What have we got to lose? So we started reading, marking, sharing.
>
> At first it was awkward. Awkward like two kids on a first date. But we stayed with it and one day, would you believe, we began to sense some good things happening. We really were starting to communicate. Like beautiful! Super! Praise the Lord!—Jerry and Beth

Texas wife:

> Result of our Bible study? It's as if we are "walking the hills together" with the third guest. It's exalting in an extraordinary way, an intimacy of spiritual togetherness. We experience a natural outpouring of feelings, a consciousness of

spiritual duet that grows steadily and imperceptibly. No way without our day-to-day studying could our exchanges flow so deep.—Lawrence and Helen

Witness from a Florida husband:

My wife and I are both employed and fortunately we can ride together to work Since it's almost forty-five minutes from our house to our jobs, we decided to put this time to good use by reading the Bible to each other. Every day we take turns driving and reading. We read a chapter or several chapters. Then we talk about what we've read. Sometimes we break in on the reading to have a deep discussion. You can't believe all the good things that have happened to our marriage since we began doing this.—Bruce and Josephine

From an Illinois husband and wife:

In our home the two of us have Bible reading each morning after breakfast. We have read the Psalms and in the New Testament, the Gospels. Recently Romans has been our inspiration. Just now it is Hebrews. We use The Living Bible and have also used the Revised Version and the King James. We each have a commentary. We have a lot of fun. We laugh and joke. We express our love for each other often, hug a lot. Fifty-nine years we've been married. That is a good long stretch. But because of our study together, we think our love and fun with great amounts of laughter keep us young. They also keep us in love with the Lord and with each other.— Harold and Alice

Chapter XIII

Thirty-Day
Trial With
Guarantee

A word in
due season,
how good it is.

In due season we shall reap if we
faint not—Galatians 6:9 (KJV).

CHALLENGE AND CLAIM

Some sage describing a speaker said, "He edified and electrified, but never specified."

Here we specify.

We challenge you to commit yourselves for thirty days trying our method. Read an agreed book of the Bible individually. Use our marks or others of your choosing. Include in this commitment at least one weekly time for discussing your marks; sharing ideas; getting acquainted; letting the Lord have His say. Talk, talk, talk. Listen, listen, listen.

And at the end of thirty days?

We guarantee you will see an improvement in your marriage.

This guarantee can be tripled if you commit yourselves for three months.

Try it.

You'll see.

Your marriage will move from ordinary to good.

From good to better

And for any couple who will continue on and on

The Lord Himself will move this marriage

From better to the very best . . .

HIS BEST!

God . . . for His great love

with which He loved us. . . .

Has made us live together with Christ. . . .

And He has raised us up with Him,

And seated us with Him in heaven.

Selections from Ephesians 2:4–6

(LAMSA).

DATE DUE